Borderlines

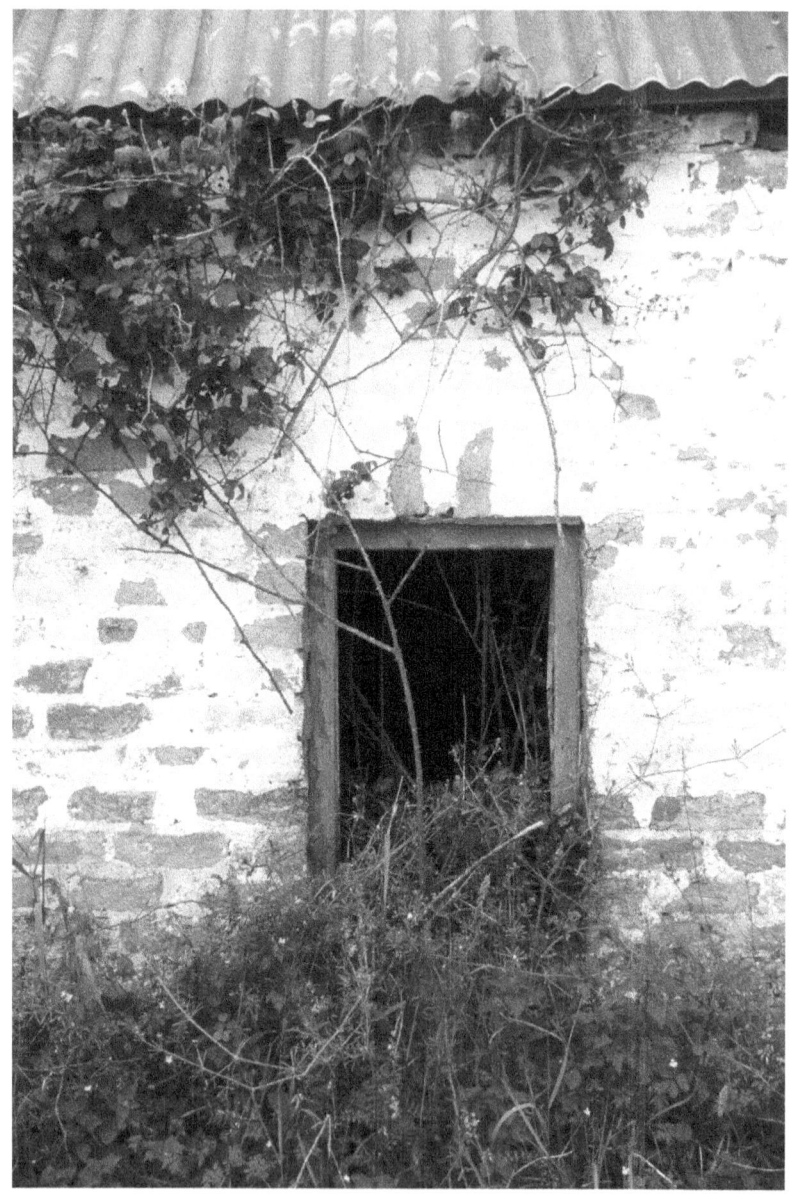

Borderlines

Vincent Woods
&
Henry Glassie

Leitrim County Council Arts Office
Carrick on Shannon
2018

First published in 2018 as part of the Iron Mountain Literature Festival by the Leitrim County Council Arts Office.

ISBN: 978-0-9576189-7-8.

Cover: "Sod of Ballymenone" by Miriam de Búrca, 2013. Vincent Woods asked the artist Miriam de Búrca to make this beautiful drawing. It depicts a sod taken from under the fallen gable wall of Hugh Nolan's house in Ballymenone, County Fermanagh.

Frontispiece: The front window of Hugh Nolan's abandoned home, 2006.

Tailpiece: The Croziers' home, north of the border in Fermanagh, 1972.

Photographs: Henry Glassie.

Design: John McGuigan and Henry Glassie.

Thanks: Philip Delamere, Pravina Shukla, Ray Cashman, Pat and Margot McCabe.

Leitrim County Council Arts Office
Áras an Contae
Carrick on Shannon
Co. Leitrim
Ireland
www.leitrimarts.ie

Contents

In remembrance

Hugh Nolan
Ballymenone, Fermanagh

Sally McKenna
Tarmon, Leitrim

Leitrim

Vincent Woods

Saint Hugh

1.

A hermit saint, Beo-Aodh—Lively Hugh,
Lived on an island in Lough Allen,
First, bright lake of the River Shannon.
Such blue he must have seen,
Such blackness of rain on the Iron Mountain,
Such eel, and drifts of swan to the hazel shore.

Like Adam after Eden,
His name seeded
In the land around
Long after his bones were laid to dust:

The lovely round sound of 'Aodh'
Becoming 'Hugh' as one language
Ceded to another,
The trace of memory held in tradition:
Son named after father, or grandfather,

The lively roll of language
Clear behind the mist of burned history.

2.

Hugh McHugh drives a blue Volkswagen:
He ferries my mother to and from the doctor,
Delivers her to the psychiatric hospital in Sligo,
Brings her home safe and sane to a wounded house.

Sometimes he'll take a glass of poteen.

His laugh was like a bubble of oxygen.

3.

Hughie Johnny was Hugh Woods,
My grandfather, pale as a ghost
And a whisper off the hundred
When he gave in:

Stoic smoker in his hard chair
By the ray-burn stove,
Flesh-shadow in the faint light.
Crippled by a broken hip
A cow's kick at seventy eight—
The bone setting crooked at home.
Never a word of complaint,
Only talk of all the hods he carried
In New York and Edinburgh.

His brown eyes glinted bright.

He loved whiskey.

4.

Hugh McPadden, his brother-in-law
Sipped gin against pain,
Waiting high up on the hill
For the doctor with his catheter
To bring relief.

From the front door he could see the lake
And the old monastery,
The graveyard which he tended like a garden,
The islands drifting like giant pike in the water.

I imagine eyes were green.

5.

He stares across the mountain to Fermanagh,
Remembers his brother James, the years
Working as a farm labourer near Enniskillen.

The hiring fairs.

Years on again, Hugh Nolan in Ballymenone
Spins the future out of dust.

6.

And you, Hugh my brother,
Stronger than Adam:
I am seven again
And my heart soars
With dint of love
As I turn the bend at Curraghs Hill
And see your car waiting.

I make the lice on my scalp
Jump for joy
As we race to find you—
Past the hazel wood,
Past the graveyard road

Past the river

The red apples shining
In the decaying orchard.

Prayer of a Farm Labourer
(or A Leitrim Man Remembers Fermanagh)

Our Father, who art in Heaven
Out of twelve, I got but seven.
Hail Mary, Full of Grace,
If I got the rest I'd leave the place.

What a young Fermanagh woman said
as she toiled with praties and fire

One day I'll walk out of here
And I'll walk and I'll walk
Until I find a ship to America
And when I land there
I'll set out again
And keep walking till I meet a man
Who has never heard of boxty

And I'll marry him

Friends

Two friends
John Woods
John Rynn
live in the same
small-big townland
farm the earth
build two houses
walk cattle to fairs
drink porter
sometimes a half-one
sign-on together
keep a sharp eye-out
for government inspectors.

John Rynn dies
He is 58

John Woods
digs his grave
smokes a pipe
in memory
raises his cap:
'God be good to him.'

25 years go by
John Rynn's son
names his son John

John Woods
gets news of a new grandson.

Strong and frail—86
he sits,
two babies
in his lap

Borderlines

Someone says:
Isn't it lovely
the turn of things—
a John Rynn and a John Woods
in the townland again

Quick as a knife
the old man says

'Two John Woods'—
You won't make dust of me yet.'

Making History

for John McCartin

A young historian is gathering stories
of the War of Independence
for a big book to commemorate a Century of Freedom.

He visits an old man whose father
fought with the IRA
But took the wrong side in the Civil War.

The young man switches on his recorder:

'I'm keen to know about the IRA shooting
of Jim Hamilton in Drumstown in June '21;
I've heard it said he was a paid informer.

Did your father ever talk about it?'

The farmer stares at the microphone,
looks out the window at the big pine tree,
slowly focuses on the earnest face
of the local teacher's son.

His voice is quiet, clear:

'O, Hamilton wasn't shot
and he was no informer.
He wasn't killed in the town, either—
but out there on that street.

They cut the head off him with a bell-hook.

We got his farm after.
My father told me all on his deathbed.

Borderlines

I say a prayer for the two of them every night,
sprinkle holy water under yon big tree—

Put that in your book,' he said
'And let them make history of it.'

Border Sod

When Bernadette McHugh was shot for singing,
Her mother was distraught, poor thing;
Near pulled down the house with dint of grief,
then went silent as the tomb.

Their farm mearned the border, one field jutted
south into Leitrim.
They used to call it Freedom Corner.

She called her sons, ordered them to dig a sod
to place in the grave with their sister,
And take a photograph, she said, to show me,

For I'll not stand to see her buried.
Patrick and Hugh dug a fine long sod—
all soft grass, moss, bothalán and nettle;

The soil was rich and brown.
They nestled it into the grave on top of her coffin.
Now, her mother said, now she'll be free to walk
Her own place, and no one will silence her.

Urn

for John Reynolds

1.

You give me
a gift
of pit-light

An urn turned
from coal and
the dust of coal

Perfect

Una gave it to you
to give to me

'Look at my arms,'
she'd say,
'Gone to nothing—

Like that poem
Vincent wrote
about his mother
and the cancer
—the watch
too big for her wrist

That's me now.

Tell him
the poems
helped
carry me.'

'O she was lovely,
Una,' you say,

'A pity
you never met her.

But she left you this:
Look at the light in it

dark-light.'

2.

You stand before me
in your kitchen whites

Your black hair crinkled
your shy eyes taking me in

Your book, you say,
Lives and Miracles—the poems—
I lent it to a friend
and it never came back

It was a gift
from my late sister
and meant a lot.

I wonder would you?

Yes, I say, I'll get you another copy.

You draw breath and give me
a master class in my own words:

'The sour-sweet smell of your uncles,
The roses spattered by the door,
The lad in the churn,

Borderlines

The bitter fellow home from England,
The Cortina crashing into the moon—

O it's all in there,'

3.

I see you, John, walking up the drumlin fields
near Fenagh with your friend who's leaving soon,
Walking up to look at 'the auld pets of cows' for one last time,
A belt tied around his rough coat, a stick in his hand.
The silence between you his way of saying goodbye.

Your voice flows to me like water from a spring
I hold out the pure-black urn
wait for the spill

Paris in a Rambling House

for Anthony Mulhern

They were discussing the French Revolution
    in McPadden's.
The new schoolteacher,
    who was boarding with them,
couldn't get over it.

Fifty years later, back for a school reunion,
    he stood looking at the ruin;
They were all inside in the kitchen, he said,
The place packed, several in rambling,
    and all debating:

One was for Marie Antoinette and the cake,
Another said every Bastille in every country
    should be pulled down,
A few said they were right, the poor,
    but there was too much bloodshed.
(That was all Danton's doing, said Myles).
One man said he'd love to have seen the Sun King
    or at least walk in the gardens of Versailles.

And I'll never forget, he said,
The old woman in the corner cut through all:

'The guillotine, the guillotine,
That's what's needed here.'

Madness

Rose Wynne went mad
One summer's morning.
Stripped off her clothes,
Right down to her skin,
Ran down the lane
From the house, ran
Right across the road
In front of the crowd
Walking to mass.

Some of them said
She was laughing
Like a wild creature,
Some said she was crying
And screaming about a man,
A man, a man

She ran straight out
In front of them
And down towards
The old nunnery.

Her father and uncle
Went off after her,
And that was that.

McPadden's hackney
Came around three,
Took her away
To the asylum in Sligo.

Mary would always remember
The shrug of the father's shoulders,
The way he raised his hat to all

And said 'Don't mind her now,
Don't mind her at all;
You go on to mass—

Won't we look after her.'

Fishing for Pike

for Beatriz

The young woman is left handed.
Her head scarf is white with flecks of ashy black.
She casts out into the lough, reels in and casts again.
In my country, she said, women fish
But not here, it seems.
I like it—it feels like you're catching time
or holding it.
Pike I do not eat, but I respect them as a foe.

And across there, she nods, another country.
Who would think it?
But the fish, they swim, they do not know these borders.

Fermanagh

Henry Glassie

The Concept of Place

My dear friend Vincent Woods, poet and playwright, gave me the topic, the concept of place. Out of my experience in Ballymenone, south of Enniskillen in the County Fermanagh, and inspired by the writings of D. W. Meinig, Yi-Fu Tuan, and W. G. Hoskins, Estyn Evans, Michael J. Murphy, and Patrick Kavanagh, I created a talk. The talk was prepared for a specific time and place, the Iron Mountain Literature Festival in Carrick on Shannon, County Leitrim, in 2017. With an audience of people from the Irish Borderland before me, I had little need to expand in explanation. The paucity of informational digressions and the incorporation of regional language serve to sustain the tone of locality; substance and style merge as Joyce taught us to do. There are no quotation marks, for I have made borrowed words my own, streamlining for oral presentation, but complete and accurate texts of the stories I used, while building a story out of stories in the manner of Faulkner and García Márquez, can be found in my books on Ballymenone—*Passing the Time* and *The Stars*—and I have added a set of readings at the end to open paths away from my text. That text follows, as given.

Ballymenone

Hugh Nolan's house stands to the right as the Rossdoney Lane runs by, dipping through the Hollow to end at the lough. His grandfather built it out of slap brick, and Hugh Nolan was born there on the day after Christmas in 1896. He lived in one of its two rooms, sleeping by night in front of the hearth, sitting by day at the corner, linking the kettle down for tea and splashing oil on the turf that smoked his home to every shade of black.

He lived with cats and went on a stick, his strong back bent by years of wheeling turf. His neighbours called him a saint. He pedaled his black bike to Mass every Sunday, first at Arney, then in Enniskillen, and he dressed like a holy hermit of old in a long black coat bound round with a purple sash.

They called him a saint and revered him as a historian. He studied in youth with Hughie McGiveney, the leading historian of the time, a poor farming man who lived with his cats and grumbling wife, just below in the Hollow.

Hugh Nolan learned, he said, by listening, to the old people talking, and, while delicately balancing the evidence, he picked up the heavy chain of transmission and carried it on to become the teller of truth for his place, Ballymenone. That's not a name found on any map, but it was known to the Four Masters, John O'Donovan found it in use in 1835, and it remained the old people's name for a clutch of townlands at the point where the Arney River flows into Upper Lough Erne.

Vincent has asked me to speak about the concept of place, of meaningful space, and I have chosen to follow

Hugh Nolan into the understanding of place once shared by the people of Ballymenone, farming folk more Catholic than Protestant, more poor than rich. Hugh Nolan is my master. I learned from him, just as he learned from Hughie McGiveney. I too listened to the old people talking, and my primary sources are the conversations that took place at his hearth between 1972, when I arrived, and 1981, the year of his death.

In place, beauty comes first. Hugh Nolan told me how a neighbour once came upon Hughie McGiveney standing on a hillside and gazing in rapture over the land. The neighbour touched Hughie, breaking the spell, and Old Hughie said—as though he were a tourist seeing the place for the first time—It's a lovely country, a lovely country altogether.

Atop Gortdonaghy Hill, in her long thatched house, Ellen Cutler looks over the half door, watching God's big picture show. That's what she called it, God's big picture show. Her eye slides down the land toward the lough. Low clouds skim by, opening a hole in the sky. A white house leaps on a field of green. The rumpled topography sharpens, then flattens in shadow. That view, she says, fills you like a feast. With beauty like that in the eye, you feel no hunger in the gut.

In the local song describing this landscape, sung in my day by Marty Crudden, Hughie McGiveney's word for his place — lovely — appears six times in twenty lines. Lough Erne's lapping waters are lovely. Devenish Island is lovely. Enniskillen is lovely. The lofty hill of Knockninny, just south of Ballymenone, has, the song says, a beauty rich and rare.

When a generation earlier, Old Hugie composed his own hymn to his place, he, like the poetic monks at the Irish dawn, praised nature:

The wild goose and the mighty swan
And other birds are known.
Twas a glorious sight to see their flight
Over the hills of Ballymenone.

Old Hughie McGiveney was a bright star and a great hand, Michael Boyle said, at stacking turf and hay. The beauty that struck him was cultural too. Earlier in his song he said:

As I walked along the Arney Road,
I thought the country grand,
With long brick hacks and big turf stacks
All through the Holy Land.

(Composed for the people of his place, Hugh Mc-Giveney's words require a touch of explanation. In the hack, handmade slap brick are drying, like turf in the clamp, and the Holy Land is a pet name for Sessiagh, a big townland west along the Arney, where only Catholics live.)

Where birds in flight and turf in the stack are both thought lovely, where nature and culture meet and mix, beauty flowers in place. During generations of experimentation, farmers find what nature wants, adjusting and adapting to discover the intentions implicit in God's creation of their environment. Then culture captures nature and workers further God's design by struggling at once toward use and beauty.

Their place, they say in Ballymenone, is not for cropping, not for the bite of the plough. It is, as it was in the time of *The Tain*, a place for cattle. On the humpy drumlins, the grass springs unbidden. That's God's gift. Then the farmers take command, splitting the fields, some for the cattle to graze, others to raise the hay that will see them

23

through the winter. The smooth green fields, the source of all profit, are lovely, right enough.

Brown bog fills the dips between the green hills, and Hugh Nolan said there was no more beautiful sight than the bog glittering with the white shirts of men, some cutting, some lifting, some wheeling the turf to the spread ground, there to be built into clamps, then lumps, then stacks. The gift of the heroic bogman, the turf will fuel the hearth where tea flows in, words flow out, the lungs are wrecked, and society is intimately built during the long night's ceili.

Of course, if you equip greedy men with advanced technology, what you will get is the violence Pope Francis decries in his magisterial Encyclical on ecology. You won't get places built; you'll get places destroyed. But if you put the earth in the hands of peasants who work the land around their dwellings with hand tools, then you will have places created, and if the tools are wielded with care and skill, the productive place is apt to be beautiful too. And so it was, not so long ago, in Mr. Nolan's Ballymenone.

In Ballymenone's own terms, the beauty of the landscape is perpetuated by ardent industry, by working people who enspirit the material by brightening the dull and smoothing the rough. There is a beauty in the bright, freshly whitewashed wall; in the gleaming rows of delph on the dresser; in the smooth, straight lines of the ridge and furrow on the moss ground; in the rows of symmetrical rooks on the meadow; in the trim hedges, hacked back with the billhook; in the long brick hacks and big turf stacks.

Beauty abides where nature and culture fuse, where need and pride meet in place. In this place, they say, you are always on the go, so you are, scrubbing muddy floors, sloughing and ploughing after the damned old cows. The closer you look at it, they say, the worse it looks, but you can't despair—despair is the worst, the very worst—so you must carry on, passing the time by brightening the dull with witty crack, smoothing the rough with the spade, and finding consolation in flashes of beauty within the tremendous dominion of the dull and rough.

Beauty of a peculiarly local sort is one definitive trait of place. History is another.

The ceili is over. Tom, the boy rebel, is gone, Johnny and Packie are back in the Hollow, Tommy the thatcher has climbed over the hill to the beautiful house he built, and I remain to wash the teapot and cups. Hugh walks with me to the door. God bless, he says, Safe home. I stand for a moment, marveling at the stars and the sweet, deep silence of a place where electricity has yet to come.

On the lane, in the dark, I am standing in history. Behind me, the lane descends to the shore, where across a strip of lough, Saint Patrick stood on Inishmore and shook his staff in my direction, saying, Ballymenone, I know you are there, but you're not worth a visit. Not worth a visit? Maybe because Ballymenone was, as it remains, unimportant. Maybe because Ballymenone's people needed no persuasion.

To my right, the land lifts to Drumbargy Brae where once stood the mansion of a middleman in the avaricious system of the landlords. His house has long been tossed, its stones carted away to build out offices for cattle.

To my left, in the days of landlords and famine, lived Mrs. Timoney, the greatest hero in Ballymenone's historical storyworld. A widow, she raised her children while doing the hard work of a woman at the hearth and the hard work of a man in the fields. With her shoes over her shoulder, she walked all the way to Ballyconnell twice a year to pay the rate on her scrap of land. Then refreshed with a noggin of gruel, she was back in the fields the next day, coping lea sod with a loy.

Ahead, the lane will sidle by the Alders, where Hughie McGiveney once met a talking cat, and then it will run on

to end at the Derrylin Road, where in 1829, on the thir-
teenth of July, because the twelfth fell on Sunday, Protestant farmers marched south to a meeting, declaring as they
passed that, on their return, they would burn to the ground
every Catholic house in Ballymenone.

(Angered, you see, by the success of brave Dan O'Con-
nell's campaign for Catholic Emancipation.)

On their return, they were met by Catholic farmers,
armed only with pitchforks, graips, and scythes. The Or-
angemen retreated up Mackan Hill and formed into line
of battle, armed with Tower muskets. When the Catholics
advanced, they fired a volley, but amateur marksmen tend
to fire high. No Catholic was harmed, though in the ensu-
ing melee three Protestant men were killed.

Hugh Nolan began his account by saying, Well, that
was a fight, unfortunately, like many other fights that took
place in this country. It was between Catholics and Prot-
estants. He went on to tell the whole tale in orderly detail,
as a historian must, maintaining objectivity over a flow of
melancholy. Michael Boyle grew excited with the crescendo
of action in his rendition. Hugh Patrick Owens proclaimed
it a glorious victory, secured through divine intervention.
Peter Flanagan thought it was a disaster.

Men of one generation who took communion at the same
altar rail, they differed in personal opinion. But all reported
the same facts, acknowledging sectarian violence and gathering
in sympathy. In sympathy, the names that survived through
a century and a half of oral tellings all belonged to the dead:
Ignatius MacManus who was hanged for the crime, though
he had done no killing, and the three Protestant men, Mealey,
Robinson, and Scarlett, who were slain in the field.

The old men paused in narration to locate the homes of
the dead Protestant men with precision. They all lived here,
right here in our place. They were neighbours. The final and
dominant commandment, constantly cited in Ballyme-

none, is to love your neighbour as yourself. And who is your neighbour, the catechism continues. All mankind.

In Ballymenone's history of conflict, in tale after tale, there lies embedded the deep structure of the Mackan Fight. Threatened or wronged, the brave must fight. Their cause being just, they will win. But in winning, they will lose, having gambled their immortal souls. In the tension of bravery and faith, there is no choice but choice.

Hugh Nolan mapped the mythic ground in his tale of Saint Columcille. From Finnian of Moville, Columcille borrowed Jerome's second translation of the Psalter that had newly come from Rome. Writing hastily through the night by a light burning from his hand, Columcille made a copy. Finnian was outraged and took his case to Diarmait, the high king. This Diarmait was kin to Columcille, but he found in favor of Finnian, saying, To every cow belongs her calf, and to every book belongs its copy.

Now it was Columcille who knew fury. A man of noble blood, he raised an army and defeated Diarmait in the battle of Cul Dreimne in Sligo in the year 561. Then, as Hugh Nolan put it, Columcille got sorry for what he'd done—it was one of the three worst acts of a saint, according to the ancient triads—and he went to the mate of his soul, Molaise, on Devenish Island in Lower Lough Erne. The penance put upon him was to go to Scotland and convert to the faith as many as had been killed in battle, and to leave Ireland and never return.

Wronged, he fought. Fighting, he won. Winning, he lost. At the age of forty-two, Columcille sailed for Scotland, and a member of the bardic order he wrote:

> There is a grey eye
> that looks back at Ireland.
> Never will it see again
> the men of Ireland or her women.

27

Columcille was Ireland's first and paradigmatic exile. Of the victors at Mackan, one was hanged, the others were transported to Van Diemen's Land, exiles too. Winning, they lost.

That's the pattern in the battle tales of Ballymenone, and that was the message the old men—rebels in youth—offered gently to the lads who played in the patriot game during the time of the Troubles, when bombs blew over the lough, soldiers prowled down the country lanes, and I was there.

While shaping their historical predicament into artful narrative, Hugh Nolan and his colleagues faced violence and united in sympathy, lamenting the dead and choking back the bad word in evaluation of their fellow flawed mortals.

Ballymenone's topical range runs from violence through questionable patriotism to sympathy for human creatures squirming on the pins of their dilemmas. I find a comparable range in the contemporary literature of Ballymenone's region—this Borderland. That literature occasionally addresses the Troubles directly, but it is always, I think, conditioned by the memories and experiences of artists who lived here in the time of the Troubles, when differences were stressed and the killings were too close, too particular.

I mean the writings of Vincent Woods, Pat McCabe, Eugene McCabe, and John McGahern. Read their works and you will find — as you would have found in the serious talk at the firesides of Ballymenone — parochial complexity, precisely sited brutality, and a pervasive human response to human difference.

In Dublin last year, copies of the Proclamation and portraits of the Rising's martyrs appeared everywhere. Informative labels made Stephen's Green into an open-air battlefield museum. In New York, my daughter, a theatre professional, Irish by identity and named for Ellen Cutler, stood on the stage of a full house on Broadway and recited from deep memory Yeats's "Easter 1916," raising up again a few names from the host of the dead.

And last year, Pat McCabe, man of Monaghan, considered a century of nationhood in *Sacrifice at Easter*, a sequence of scenes spun around an old fort in Cork. There's no published text; you had to be there. The play begins with a gamble, ends in orphanage, and comes home to this Borderland, climaxing in two red-lit, sacrificial, crucifixional moments of profound sympathy—one for a murdered Protestant farmer, one for a young IRA volunteer.

Like Vincent's *At the Black Pig's Dyke*, Pat's *Sacrifice at Easter* is a masterpiece of Borderland drama, documenting the historical times through which we have come toward understanding.

To be useful, history need not be contrived out of grand and noble deeds. It needs only to be human. And when history is not distanced from us by chronology, but located here among our damp hills, set spatially and vitalized in art, then, like working the land, historical understanding converts a slice of space into a place—a place worth defending and occupying—a home.

Beauty, then history, then home. So, how are things at home? Hugh Nolan tells us:

This John O'Prey was at home in Cavan when he was struck with a fine idea. He would set a bench by the roadside, put a rifle on it, and then lean comfortably back on a ditch. And he'd have a box of cartridges beside him, and all he'd have to do was to keep firing shots away while the cartridges lasted. And it didn't make any matter who passed up or down—man, woman, or beast—well, let them take the consequences.

The neighbours got wind of John's plan and reported him to the Gards, so when he went to the station to get a license for the rifle, as any law-abiding man about to slay his neighbours would do, his application was denied. Outraged at this injustice (like Columcille, say), John resorted to kicking.

An old man was standing after Mass at the chapel gate, filling his pipe for a relaxing smoke. John kicked him. Pipe, tobacco, and matches flew in all directions. He met two fellows on bicycles. He kicked them, and they kicked him. And things like that went on for a month or so. It was a thing that was going on daily. John was a-kicking every time he went out.

So then, the crowds joined together for a while's kicking at him. And one crowd took position on the road, and another in the field, and they used to kick him back and forth over the hedge. That went on till there came a throng of work, and the people quit coming. And he was lying in the field all the time, night and day. So, damn it, one day, sore as he was, he stood up and found he could walk.

That's how it is at home, where, as Patrick Kavanagh explains, hating one's neighbours is a tenet in the small farmer's religion. Kicked black by his neighbours, but still able to move, John O'Prey left his old home and went in search of a new one.

So then, how fares the one who gets up and goes? Hugh Nolan tells us:

This George Armstrong, he lived in a little house in Gortdonaghy, down at the foot of the hill. Mrs. Cutler's house, do you see, would be way up on the top of the hill.

Well, George went away to Australia in his young days. And he was doing the best, making plenty of money. But there started a disease; they call it cholera. It's going in foreign counties still. So, he was very bad with it, and he thought he was going to die. Finally, he started to mend, and he got so that he was able to get to his feet and get out.

(Able to walk, like John O'Prey at home in Cavan, George Armstrong got up and got out.)

30

He took ship in Australia, dreaming on the voyage home of a cow's grass of good land and a rood of the best turf bog that ever a man stuck a spade in. George landed in Derry, made his way to Enniskillen, weighing three pounds, three pence in his pocket. When he got home, he was so light that his step made no sound on the street.

He stood at the door. The mother was doing something at the fire, and when she turned around and saw him, she nearly lost her life at the appearance of him. She picked him up, wrapped him in white cloth—an infant's swaddling, a corpse's shroud—and put him in a wee basket beside the fire.

The rumor went out about the country that George was home. When the people came to see him, there was so sign of George, and some of them asked, Where is George at the present time?

She went and lifted the wee basket, took the cloth from over him.

And they looked in.

At that, his story told, Hugh Nolan let the laughter roll out of control.

Funny as the stories are, he said, there bes a warning in them. No earthly place is perfect. Stay home, and the neighbours will kick you black. Leave, and you will diminish to the limit of human failure—a wee thing in a basket, unable to move or speak.

George Armstrong wound up like the Cumaean Sybil who was granted a wish in exchange for sex when Apollo wanted to bed her. She asked to live a thousand years, but neglected to ask for perpetual youth and became, as the ages passed, a shriveled thing in a bottle.

George was even more like the Unnamable at the end of Samuel Beckett's great trilogy—a sentient thing stuck in a pot. In a basket, a bottle, a pot—or up to the neck in sand—the human abides in a being next to nothingness.

With nothingness in the offing, and nothing to be done, we pass the time.

Ballymenone's humour of blackened hyperbole matches the extremes of wretchedness that wrench a laugh out of Beckett's writing. It's a stretch, sure, but there could be a connection. When Beckett was a scholar and athlete at Portora, he would often have walked across the western bridge into town. Coming down the Church Brae, he would have passed Blake's of the Hollow on his right. That's where Hughie McGiveney took his drink when he came to the cattle mart, entertaining the men at the bar with the tall tales of extravagant distress and collapse, called pants in Ballymenone. Sam might have entered, listened, laughed, and learned.

Probably not, but it remains a fact that Ballymenone's sense of humour and Samuel Beckett's run close, something witty, brave, and wistful about it all.

At home, in place, working the land by day and telling tales in the ceili at night, they strive for brightness in the vast ambit of the dull, and they ingeniously drive their failures past possibility, gallantly making a joke out of the whole damn thing.

Sources and Readings

Aalen, F. H. A., Kevin Whelan, and Matthew Stout. *Atlas of the Irish Rural Landscape*. Cork: Cork University Press, 2011 [1997].

Anderson, Alan Orr, and Marjorie Ogilvie Anderson. *Adomnan's Life of Columba*. London: Thomas Nelson, 1961.

Beckett, Samuel. *Waiting for Godot*. New York: Grove Press, 1954.

———. *Molloy*. New York: Grove Press, 1955.

———. *Malone Dies*. New York: Grove Press, 1956.

———. *The Unnamable*. New York: Grove Press, 1958.

———. *Happy Days*. New York: Grove Press, 1961.

Bullock, Shan F. *The Loughsiders*. London: Harrap, 1924.

Carney, James. *Medieval Irish Lyrics: Selected and Translated*. Berkeley: University of California Press, 1967.

Carson, Ciaran. *The Tain*. London: Penguin, 2007.

Cashman, Ray. *Storytelling on the Northern Irish Border: Characters and Community*. Bloomington: Indiana University Press, 2008.

———.*Packy Jim: Folklore and Worldview on the Irish Border*. Madison: University of Wisconsin Press, 2016.

Chrétien, Douglas. *The Battle Book of the O'Donnells*. Berkeley: University of California Press, 1935.

Danaher, Kevin. *The Pleasant Land of Ireland*. Cork: Mercier Press, 1970.

Day, Angélique, and Patrick McWilliams, eds. *Ordnance Survey Memoirs of Ireland, Volume Four: Parishes of County Fermanagh I, 1834-5: Enniskillen and Upper Lough Erne.* Belfast: Institute of Irish Studies, 1990.

De Paor, Louis, ed. *Leabhar na hAthghabhála: Poems of Repossession.* Hexham: Broadaxe Books, 2016.

Evans, E. Estyn. *Mourne Country: Landscape and Life in South Down.* Dundalk: Dundalgan Press, 1967 [1951].

————. *The Personality of Ireland: Habitat, Heritage and History.* Cambridge: Cambridge University Press, 1973.

————. *Ireland and the Atlantic Heritage: Selected Writings.* Dublin: Lilliput Press, 1996.

Gailey, Alan. *Rural Houses of the North of Ireland.* Edinburgh: John Donald, 1984.

Gallagher, Bryan. *Barefoot in Mullyneeny: A Boy's Journey Towards Belonging.* London: HarperCollins, 2005.

Gallagher, Joseph, and Greg Stevenson. *Traditional Cottages of County Donegal.* Glencolmcille: Under the Thatch, 2012.

Glassie, Henry. *All Silver and No Brass: An Irish Christmas Mumming.* Dublin: The Dolmen Press, 1976.

————. *Passing the Time in Ballymenone: Culture and History of an Ulster Community.* Philadelphia: University of Pennsylvania Press, 1982.

————. *Irish Folktales.* New York: Pantheon, 1985.

————. *The Stars of Ballymenone.* Bloomington: Indiana University Press, 2016 [2006].

Hansen, William. *The Book of Greek and Roman Folktales, Legends, and Myths.* Princeton: Princeton University Press, 2017.

Healy, Dermot. *A Goat's Song*. New York: Viking, 1994.

Heaney, Seamus. *Door into the Dark*. London: Faber and Faber, 1972 [1969].

———. *Field Work*. New York: Farrar Straus Giroux, 1979.

———. *Sweeney Astray*. Derry: Field Day, 1983.

Hoskins, W. G. *The Making of the English Landscape*. London: Hodder and Stoughton, 1955.

———. *English Landscapes*. London: British Broadcasting Corporation, 1973.

Kavanagh, Patrick. *The Green Fool*. London: Martin Brian and O'Keeffe, 1971 [1938].

———. *Tarry Flynn*. London: The Pilot Press, 1948.

———. *Collected Pruse*. London: Martin Brian and O'Keeffe, 1973.

Kavanagh, Peter, ed. *The Complete Poems of Patrick Kavanagh*. New York: Peter Kavanagh Hand Press, 1972.

Kiely, Benedict. *Proxopera: A Tale of Modern Ireland*. Boston: David R. Godine, 1980.

Kinsella, Thomas. *The Tain*. Dublin: The Dolmen Press, 1969.

———. *Butcher's Dozen*. Dublin: Peppercanister, 1972.

Knowlson, James. *Damned to Fame: The Life of Samuel Beckett*. New York: Simon and Schuster, 1996.

Livingstone, Peadar. *The Fermanagh Story*. Enniskillen: Cumann Seanchais Chlochair, 1969.

Maxwell, Marion, and Fiona Wright. *Making It Home: The Resettlement of WWI Ex-Servicemen on Cleenish Island in Upper Lough Erne*. Belfast: Bellanaleck Local History Group, 2017.

McCabe, Eugene. *Heritage and Other Stories*. London: Victor Gollancz, 1978.

———. *Death and Nightingales*. London: Vintage, 1998 [1992].

———. *Tales from the Poorhouse*. Loughcrew: Gallery Press, 1999.

McCabe, Patrick. *The Butcher Boy*. New York: Fromm International, 1993.

———. *Breakfast on Pluto*. New York: HarperCollins, 1998.

———. *Call Me the Breeze*. New York: HarperCollins, 2003.

———. *The Stray Sod Country*. New York: Bloomsbury, 2010.

———. *Hello Mr Bones, Goodbye Mr Rat*. London: Quercus, 2013.

———. *Heartland*. Stillorgan: New Island Books, 2018.

McCarthy, Ted. *November Wedding and Other Poems*. Dublin: Lilliput Press, 1998.

McGahern, John. *Amongst Women*. London: Faber and Faber, 1990.

———. *Memoir*. London: Faber and Faber, 2005.

Meinig, D.W., ed. *The Interpretation of Ordinary Landscapes: Geographical Essays*. New York: Oxford University Press, 1979.

Montague, John. *The Rough Field*. Dublin: The Dolmen Press, 1974.

Muldoon, Paul. *Rising to the Rising*. Loughcrew: Gallery Press, 2016.

Murphy, Gerard. *Early Irish Lyrics: Eighth to Twelfth Century*. Oxford: Oxford University Press, 1970 [1956].

Murphy, Michael J. *At Slieve Gullion's Foot*. Dundalk: Dundalgan Press, 1940.

———. *Tyrone Folk Quest*. Belfast: Blackstaff Press, 1973.

Ní Dhomnail, Nuala. *Selected Poems*. Michael Hartnett, trans. Dublin: Raven Arts Press, 1988.

Ó Catháin, Séamus, and Patrick O'Flanagan. *The Living Landscape: Kilgalligan, Eris, County Mayo*. Dublin: Comhairle Bhéaloideas Éireann, 1975.

O'Donnell, Manus. *The Life of Colum Cille*. Brian Lacey, ed. Dublin: Four Courts Press, 1998.

O'Donovan, John. *Annals of the Kingdom of Ireland By the Four Masters, From the Earliest Period to the Year 1616*. 7 vols. Dublin: Hodges, Smith, 1856.

O'Toole, Fintan. *The Lie of the Land: Irish Identities*. London: Verso, 1997.

Pope Francis. *Laudato Si': On Care for Our Common Home*. Encyclical Letter. Vatican City: Libreria Editrice Vaticana, 2015.

Stephens, James. *The Insurrection in Dublin*. New York: Macmillan, 1916.

Synge, John M. *The Aran Islands*. Dublin: Maunsel, 1906.

Tuan, Yi-Fu. *Space and Place: The Perspective of Experience*. Minneapolis: University of Minnesota Press, 1977.

Williams, Raymond. *Border Country*. London: Chatto and Windus, 1978 [1960].

Woods, Vincent. "At the Black Pig's Dyke," in John Fairleigh, ed. *Far from the Land: Contemporary Irish Plays*. London: Methuen Drama, 1998, pp. 1-61.

———. *Lives and Miracles*. Galway: Arlen House, 2002.

———. *A Cry from Heaven*. London: Methuen Drama, 2005.

———. *Leaves of Hungry Grass: Poetry and Ireland's Great Hunger*. Hamden: Ireland's Great Hunger Museum, Quinnipiac University Press, 2016.

Yeats, W. B. *Later Poems*. New York: Macmillan, 1924.

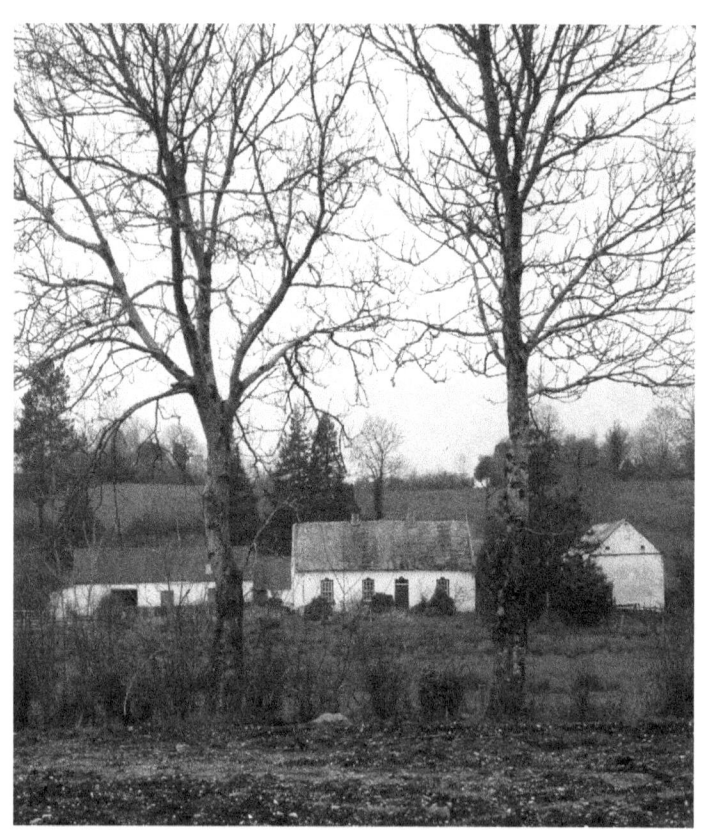

www.ingramcontent.com/pod-product-compliance
Lightning Source LLC
Chambersburg PA
CBHW072301170526
45158CB00003BA/1136